IMAGES
of America

NORTH
MYRTLE BEACH

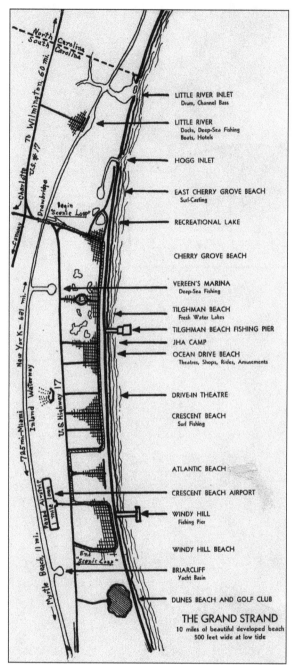

The area encompassing North Myrtle Beach appears on a 1950 brochure entitled "The Grand Strand." Beginning at the map's northernmost point, the four municipalities consolidated into North Myrtle Beach in 1968 were Cherry Grove Beach, Ocean Drive Beach, Crescent Beach, and Windy Hill Beach. Between Crescent and Windy Hill Beaches lies Atlantic Beach, a predominantly Black town that incorporated in 1966 but chose to remain independent from the North Myrtle Beach consolidation two years later. (Author's collection.)

ON THE COVER: Roberts Pavilion, pictured here around 1936, was the scene of this multigenerational photograph likely representing a grandmother, mother, and granddaughter preserving the memory of their visit to Ocean Drive Beach not long after this pavilion opened. Serving as a catalyst for development of Ocean Drive and nearby beach communities, this pavilion offered lively entertainment, ocean access, and an opportunity to meet new friends, all of which were largely absent in rural North and South Carolina counties within a reasonable driving distance. These beach vacationers' names have been lost to history, but the memories created while they were visiting Ocean Drive in its infancy likely lasted throughout their lives. (Author's collection.)

IMAGES
of America

NORTH
MYRTLE BEACH

Susan Hoffer McMillan

ARCADIA
PUBLISHING

Published by Arcadia Publishing
Charleston, South Carolina

Library of Congress Control Number: 2020948562

For all general information, please contact Arcadia Publishing:
Telephone 843-853-2070
Fax 843-853-0044
E-mail sales@arcadiapublishing.com
For customer service and orders:
Toll-Free 1-888-313-2665

Visit us on the Internet at www.arcadiapublishing.com

This book is dedicated to the late Connelly Burgin Berry (1919–2007)—land surveyor; historian; chairman of Vereen Memorial Historical Gardens committee; charter member and chairman of Horry County Historic Preservation Commission; charter president of the Horry County Historical Society; charter Crescent Beach town councilman; twice-elected Crescent Beach mayor; author of *Berry's Blue Book, A Book of Historical Interviews*; freelance writer of historical articles for various periodicals; Southeastern Commercial College graduate; Cheraw High School class of 1937 graduate and reunion organizer; and resident for 57 years in the home he built for his wife and daughters at Crescent Beach (which is now within North Myrtle Beach).

CONTENTS

ACKNOWLEDGMENTS

This author was blessed with personal writings and history books from the late C. Burgin Berry's extensive historical archives that were provided by his daughters Sandy Berry Nettles, Bobbie Berry Lackey, and Cissy Berry. These materials, especially *Berry's Blue Book, A Book of Historical Interviews*, by C.B. Berry, were invaluable in researching North Myrtle Beach's history and will support future research. Other assistance came from Selden B. "Bud" Hill, director emeritus of the Village Museum in McClellanville, South Carolina, and Polly Lowman, editor and publisher of the *North Myrtle Beach Times*.

Unless otherwise noted, all images are from the author's lifetime collection, which she amassed after having spent a childhood vacationing regularly at Ocean Drive, Cherry Grove, and Windy Hill Beaches. After college, the author relocated to the Grand Strand has lived nearby for five decades and counting.

INTRODUCTION

This is a 20th-century history of North Myrtle Beach, South Carolina, with references to 19th-century events. Cherry Grove, Ocean Drive, Crescent, and Windy Hill Beaches began as small residential communities that incorporated separately but chose to merge as tourism blossomed. North Myrtle Beach became the name of the new city on March 26, 1968. Atlantic Beach, Little River, and Chestnut Hill (formerly Vaught), established around 1895, are neighboring communities with distinct histories not featured in this book due to space constraints. Also significant is Waties Island, located immediately north of North Myrtle Beach and granted to emigrant fur trader William Waties following his 1694 landing at Charleston, South Carolina.

The name of Cherry Grove Beach derives from the indigenous cherry trees on the nearby Cherry Grove plantation, established around 1735. Incorporated on March 26, 1959, the town began with council members Nicholas Foy Nixon, John Legrande "Happy" Vereen, R. Marvin Edge, K.V. McLeod, and Mayor Charles Duffy "Charlie" Nixon. It is now the Cherry Grove section of North Myrtle Beach.

Ocean Drive Beach (formerly Ocean Drive Estates) incorporated on June 8, 1948, became the Ocean Drive section of North Myrtle Beach in 1968 while retaining its status as the apex of four consolidated beach towns. Upon incorporation, its citizens elected councilmen James Blakeney Jackson, A.M. Rush, James B. Harris, Hardy S. Bennett, and Mayor Luther W. Fenegan. Two years later, dial telephone service began. Ocean Drive is renowned for the shag, South Carolina's official state dance, and for two hometown celebrities—*Wheel of Fortune's* Vanna White and the Golf Channel's Kelly Tilghman (now retired).

Crescent Beach (formerly the Ward Estate) incorporated in 1953 with councilmen J.O. Baldwin, Connelly Burgin Berry, Richard K. Cartrette, Harry Livingston, and Mayor James Wardlaw Perrin. Named for the strand's crescent shape, this town gave North Myrtle Beach its first mayor when Crescent Beach's mayor of 12 years, Robert L. Edge Sr., was chosen to lead the new city. The Grand Strand Airport and adjacent Beachwood Golf Club are area landmarks west of Highway 17.

Windy Hill Beach, at the southern end of North Myrtle Beach, was noted for high sand dunes when George Washington passed through in 1791, but they gradually eroded. Incorporated on October 10, 1964, this town is located on property that previously belonged to the William R. Lewis family of Conway, South Carolina. The charter council members were Charles W. Byers, P.K. Fleming, W. Leamon Todd, David B. Witherspoon Jr., and Mayor John T. Harrell.

North Myrtle Beach encompasses an area earlier called the Grand Strand—a term that now encompasses South Carolina's coastline from Little River to Georgetown. This clever name, created by publicist Claude Dunnagan of Ocean Drive Beach, attracted interest from the Myrtle Beach Chamber of Commerce, which led to the chamber purchasing its name rights from Dunnagan. With expanded marketing coverage, the 60-mile Grand Strand is now recognized worldwide.

The area encompassing North Myrtle Beach has experienced impressive growth and development in the last century. In 2018, North Myrtle Beach celebrated 50 years as a city. Drag races and airplane landings on its strand are now history. Beach music, originally a mid-20th-century teen music craze, established a home in Ocean Drive Beach via the Society of Stranders, giving shag dancing and Ocean Drive international fame. The North Myrtle Beach Museum, the city's newest historical asset, has been celebrating and preserving area history since 2013.

A nine-and-a-half-foot shark weighing over 300 pounds was caught from the Cherry Grove Fishing Pier by Columbia, South Carolina, fisherman Jim Michie in the 1960s. A weekend shark fisherman who later became an archaeologist, Michie spent all weekend on the pier—alternately fishing and sleeping—before hooking his prized shark. Michie also taught Walter Maxwell how to fish for sharks and built the reel Maxwell used that resulted in the world-record tiger shark Maxwell caught here in 1964 (see page 15). Pier fishing for sharks grew in popularity until it interfered with normal pier fishing, so it is no longer allowed on Grand Strand fishing piers.

One

CHERRY GROVE BEACH

Cherry Grove Beach From the Air, Cherry Grove, S. C.

Cherry Grove Beach was a village around 1950. The beachfront row is sparse, and only one car occupies the main street named Sea Mountain Highway. In 1859, Cherry Grove Plantation's 9,940 acres were sold by Col. Daniel W. Jordan to Nicholas N. Nixon, whose heirs began developing it in the 1920s. The Jordans moved to Laurel Hill Plantation, now within Brookgreen Gardens in Murrells Inlet, South Carolina, and later to Camden, South Carolina, where Jordan family descendants remain.

Little Naples Restaurant was a mid-20th-century Italian American family restaurant specializing in seafood, chicken, steak, chops, and spaghetti. It also served breakfast. It was near the Highway 17 drawbridge on the Sea Mountain Highway leading into Cherry Grove Beach. Owners Harry B. and Lorena Buffkin ran this popular restaurant with a private dining room for special events.

By 1969, business was increasing in the Cherry Grove section of the newly incorporated North Myrtle Beach. Multistory oceanfront hotels dot the coast; two piers are present, although the distant Inlet Pier is barely visible; and an inland water tower overlooks its expanding service area. Wooded areas between houses would soon be reduced as the pace of development accelerated.

Boulineau's Food Store, shown above in 1970, operates at 212 Sea Mountain Highway. Opened in 1948 as a community grocery, Boulineau's repeatedly expanded while opening new local businesses and acquiring established ones. Boulineau's now includes an IGA grocery store, a cafeteria with a deli, a Shell gas station/convenience store with a car wash, an ACE hardware store, and more. Boulineau's has been consecutively owned by three generations of Frank Boulineaus. The Barnacle Gift Shop (below) at 2311 North Ocean Boulevard is another Boulineau-owned enterprise. It sells beach supplies and nautical souvenirs. Similar local beachwear shops exploded in popularity in the second half of the 20th century. As they grew progressively larger, the stores preferred locations on Highway 17, where they engaged in fiercely competitive price wars. Loss leaders such as $1 beach towels attracted huge crowds of vacationers.

Surf seining season runs from the full moon in June until November but generally began locally after Labor Day, when the vacationers went home. In surf seining, a crew of strong men pulls an elongated haul net through the surf and drags it ashore. The net, filled with fish, becomes increasingly heavier as it is hauled onto the beach. However, it must be distanced from the surf so a rising tide does not reclaim any of the catch.

Cherry Grove Manor, Cherry Grove Beach, S. C.

This is the original Cherry Grove Manor as it looked around the 1940s. It was described as a modern hotel in which every room had an ocean view and a private bath. The Category 4 Hurricane Hazel played havoc with this hotel on October 15, 1954, removing its roof and third floor. The surviving two floors were sold and moved across Ocean Boulevard for restoration under a new name. Almost 50 years later, around 2000, the restored hotel was razed.

The oceanfront Cherry Grove Manor was a grander structure after it was rebuilt following Hurricane Hazel, with twin additions on opposing sides and at the back creating symmetry. Located a mile east of the intersection of Highways 17 and 9, the manor was described as a "hotel" from June through August and a "deluxe motor court" during fall and spring; it was closed in winter. M.E. Pfaff and Ralph and Vera Hellmer were the owner-operators of its 44 units and dining room.

A sunrise departure for this fishing boat with long oars indicates that a commercial seining net is about to be positioned for a hearty catch. Seining nets ranged up to a half mile in length and required regular repairs to remain effective. Commercial seining began farther south on the Grand Strand but shifted to north strand sites as development overwhelmed its earlier locations.

The Holiday House Motel at 3600 North Ocean Boulevard, shown in 1967, replaced a nearby Holiday House operated as early as 1950 by resident managers Ruth and Bob Bynum. The new motel, located immediately north of the Cherry Grove Fishing Pier, was owned by Edward Walter Prince Jr. and his wife, Margaret Suggs Prince of Loris, South Carolina, and was also managed by the Bynums. Its amenities included golf and fishing pier privileges.

Realtor John H. Nye opened Cherry Grove Fishing Pier at 3500 North Ocean Boulevard in 1950. Its success was promising due to its proximity to the Cherry Grove Inlet that divided Cherry Grove Beach from East Cherry Grove Beach (previously the barrier Futch Island). However, this inlet was closed that same year to create more marketable real estate. The pier is now part of the Prince Resort, which was built in the pier's former parking lot and extends north of there.

Cherry Grove Fishing Pier is renowned for a world-record tiger shark caught by Walter Maxwell of Columbia, South Carolina, on June 14, 1964. This trophy shark weighed 1,780 pounds on the day after it was caught, as a full day passed before a certified scale could be located for weighing it. Maxwell's world record was shattered in 2004, when a shark weighing about six additional pounds was caught in Australia.

The Ship Ahoy Motel replaced several oceanfront beach houses when it was built around 1969 at 3400 North Ocean Boulevard, immediately south of the Cherry Grove Fishing Pier. Vacationers liked swimming pools, so sand dunes were often replaced with a pool, as shown here. Ken and Doreen Rogers operated this oceanfront motel with 30 units. An earlier Ship Ahoy Motel, operated by W.T. Gowans, was located nearby around 1950.

The crowded Inlet Fishing Pier on Cherry Grove Beach's north end near Hog Inlet was 1,000 feet long. Owned and managed by J.A. Goodson, it featured a tackle shop and grill with patio dining. A swift tidal current at the mouth of the inlet attracted large fish seeking smaller fish to eat, all of which benefited the fishing sport. Due to hurricanes, this pier no longer exists.

Looking west in 1983, this aerial view of dense condominium housing shows extensive development crowding Hog Inlet's fragile ecosystem. The opposing interests of environmentalists and developers were both considered in permitting this development, but the developers ultimately won.

A second aerial view, looking east in 1983, of Hog Inlet's condominium housing shows Inlet Point from an inland perspective. Before housing crowded this point, beachgoers often came here to wade across the inlet at low tide and explore the barrier Waties Island. It was critical that these explorers returned to the mainland before a rising tide—accompanied by swift inlet currents—made crossings treacherous, as drownings have occurred here.

Inlet Fishing Pier is shown here in a view from its parking lot. The nearby Inlet Motel, operated by Bob Adams around 1950 (but not pictured here), was convenient for avid fishermen. Adams also sold and serviced refrigerators in the area. Because hospitality employment positions were seasonal, workers had other jobs to supplement their income, which resulted in countless skills and professions being represented among local hospitality staff.

The Jolly Roger and Jo-To-Mata Apartments were owned by Dr. Dayton Stokes Altman Sr. and his wife, Rosa Belle Witherspoon Altman, of Mullins, South Carolina. Following Dr. Altman's death in 1945, Rosa lived here and continued managing the apartments into her nineties, with assistance from her adult sons as needed. Afterward, she went on to become a centenarian.

North Myrtle Beach is often labeled the "World's Widest Beach" in marketing materials. This 1960s aerial view of Cherry Grove Beach illustrates its broad expanse at low tide, which can also be seen in other North Myrtle Beach locations. The span between the high and low tide lines was up to 500 feet in the 20th century. Gradually rising sea levels have since decreased beach widths.

A section of the 3,000-mile Intracoastal Waterway parallels the Atlantic Ocean approximately west of its coastal development. Here, undeveloped marshlands and woodlands enhance the natural beauty of the waterway extending alongside North Myrtle Beach. Safe inland passage for marine traffic along the East Coast connects via rivers wherever possible and was otherwise machine-dug, with its final East Coast span completed at nearby Socastee, South Carolina, in 1936.

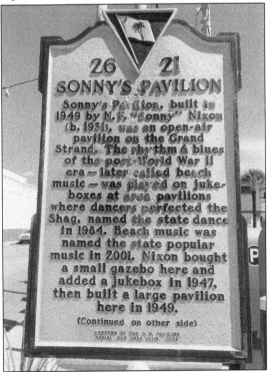

Sonny's Pavilion, built in 1949, is honored with this historical marker at the square in downtown Cherry Grove Beach. Built by local Nicholas Foy "Sonny" Nixon, the popular open-air dance venue was a place where shaggers could literally dance the night away. A victim of Hurricane Hazel in 1954, it was rebuilt and endured until the 1970s, when the structure was repurposed only to be finally destroyed by Hurricane Hugo in 1989.

Early channel lot development replaced salt marshes with a wide expanse of flat, cleared land. In this image, original channel houses appear ready for occupancy; more houses soon followed to complete this channel row development offering quick ocean access. Decades later, most of these channels had accumulated silt that rendered them too shallow for boat traffic, necessitating costly dredging in 2016 and 2017.

Mar-Lane Motel was operated by Esther H. Anderson as early as 1950 and was rebuilt after Hurricane Hazel. Efficiency apartments in this oceanfront motel slept up to eight people when it was owned and managed by Mr. and Mrs. Lane R. Wagner in the 1960s, as shown here.

The oceanfront Surf Motel, owned by Phillip R. Permenter, had a memorable post office address: Box No. 1, Cherry Grove Beach. Its modern amenities included television, air-conditioning, wall-to-wall carpet, and efficiency apartment units with electric kitchens. This motel's name was memorable too, because beach vacationers were all about the surf.

Watson's Duplex was an oceanfront rental owned by Hoyt Watson of Florence, South Carolina. Shown here around 1950, the duplex lacked landscaping—likely the result of high winds and ocean surge destroying natural vegetation during hurricanes. Extreme high winds also usually damage or topple trees. The legendary hurricane of 1893 cleared the undeveloped Grand Strand of trees and ground cover for up to 1,000 feet inland (in heavily impacted areas).

VJ's Motel, shown in the 1960s, was a colorful second-row property three blocks north of Cherry Grove Beach's downtown area. Operated by owner V.J. Arnette and later by Harry Nix, this two-story motel was on Ocean Boulevard at Twenty-seventh Avenue North and was still active in 1975.

In this view looking north from the vicinity of the Cherry Grove Fishing Pier after the removal of Hurricane Hazel debris, oceanfront redevelopment appears in stark contrast to its presently dense inhabitation. During that historic hurricane, Cherry Grove lost 300 of its 450 houses. Gauging from the crowded pier and parking lot shown here, fishing was excellent on this clear day.

"ARDLUSSA"

"On Ocean Front," Cherry Grove Beach, S. C.

Ardlussa Cottage, built around 1930, was an oceanfront rental located about midway between Cherry Grove Beach's pier and downtown. It was named for a Scottish estate and built by Daniel Hatcher Watkins. Mrs. J.H. Rivers became Ardlussa's owner-manager. Nicknamed the "house of slamming doors," Ardlussa was destroyed by Hurricane Hazel and replaced by the Sand Castle Motel, which is also now gone.

Bessent and Bell Realty in Cherry Grove Beach managed rentals for the nearby Henry Lee Apartments. The mature trees shown here suggest that the Henry Lee was located several rows inland from the beach, which generally lacked trees due to periodic hurricanes. These 12 brick apartments were rented by the week or the month.

Life is a beach when one's summer job is lifeguarding. Of course, there are beach equipment rentals to juggle and an occasional lifesaving rescue to perform while sunbathers watch closely, but it is all in a day's work. Beach rental services contract with municipalities to provide certified lifeguards along the beachfront during the summer season in exchange for exclusive rights to rent rafts, chairs, and umbrellas on the strand.

A Category 4 hurricane when it came ashore, Connie destroyed the ground floor of this oceanfront Cherry Grove Beach house on August 11, 1955. The concrete block wall collapsed from the ocean's surge undermining its foundation. Interior paneling also yielded to the menacing surf. The downstairs rooms were swept clear of furniture, while the exposed upstairs rooms reveal furniture still remaining. Hurricane Connie's highest winds measured a whopping 137 miles per hour.

The Hartford C. Motor Inn offered oceanfront apartments at Thirty-first Avenue in Cherry Grove Beach. A swimming pool replaced sand dunes and appeared to extend onto the beach, but a bulkhead stabilized the raised pool. Ada P. Dew owned this property. The name of her motel was trimmed when it acquired a new address at 5310 Ocean Boulevard. Lacy and Nancy Harris managed the Hartford Motor Inn's 55 units in 1991.

Cherry Grove Beach's extreme width at low tide is showcased in this picture with the Cherry Grove Fishing Pier in the background. Native Americans enjoyed these beaches before European settlers arrived to displace the Indigenous people. Just above this beach, on Waties Island, archaeological evidence indicates that Native Americans cooked shellfish over wood fires. Similar evidence noted at Cherry Grove Beach was erased by development.

Early channel lots created desirable housing sites with direct water access, as shown in this aerial photograph taken in the 1960s. The channels on the right are partially developed, while the newer channels on the left were yet to be surveyed as lots. John H. Nye, of Cherry Grove Realty Company, led the sales of these lots, which were copied from Florida developers who successfully created buildable canal lots in their lowlands.

Houses were more numerous on channel lots by the 1970s as compared to a few years earlier (as shown in the previous image). Bulkheads installed at the expense of homeowners helped to maintain waterfront property, while narrow lot widths allowed for the creation of the maximum number of marketable lots. When they are fully developed, multiple channel rows in close proximity form dense residential neighborhoods.

Located a stone's throw from the Inlet Fishing Pier, the Tarte Motel is pictured in 1966. Jack and Lil Woltman owned and operated this motel that promised restful privacy with views of the Intracoastal Waterway and the ocean from efficiency apartments that could sleep as many as six people. A decade later, J. Milton Webb managed this second-row Ocean Boulevard motel.

This unidentified fisherman posed in 1925 with his Penn 16/0 reel on which he caught a 44-pound king mackerel at Cherry Grove Beach. It undoubtedly was a proud day for this angler—an event worthy of a photograph preserving his trophy catch for posterity. Fishing is still a key attraction in North Myrtle Beach, especially in the Cherry Grove section, with its pier fishing and surf casting options.

This aerial view shows development between Hog Inlet and Inlet Fishing Pier. In the foreground, its gradual development is pictured shortly before the Florida-style canal lots were replicated locally. Named East Cherry Grove Beach, this property was previously called Futch Island on early area maps. The Futch family lived through a night of terror in 1893, when a hurricane that predated named storms washed over the entire island, flooding their home and cemetery.

Palmetto Shores Marina and canal lots originated in 1964, marketed by marina president John H. Nye, of Cherry Grove Realty Company. Flossie Chestnut was the marina's secretary and treasurer. This is now an established neighborhood of custom homes on canals that provide direct water access for homeowners. Accessed by land via Little River Neck Road to Coquina Drive, the Palmetto Shores subdivision connects with the Intracoastal Waterway at the former Palmetto Shores Marina store and office, which opened in 1964 and was later renamed Anchor Marina. The original store is now Captain Archie's bar and grill. Renamed yet again in 2019, the business is now Cherry Grove Marina and occupies a modern facility at 2201 Little River Road.

Lulled by the ocean's calming sounds, this unidentified fisherman may have been dreaming about the fish dinner he would enjoy after his day spent on the Cherry Grove Fishing Pier in 1972. Names carved into the pier's shelter behind him attest to others who also passed idle hours here; visitors occasionally brought sleeping bags to stay overnight in the pier's shelter when fish were biting.

The Mac-B-Anne Apartments were located one block from the beach and were promoted by noting the location's convenience to the nearby post office, drugstore, grocer, and pavilion in downtown Cherry Grove. Town council member K.V. McLeod was the contact for reservations in the apartments' air-conditioned units that slept up to five people.

Cherry Grove Beach erosion endangered oceanfront houses by 1983, as high tides progressively invaded primary dunes. Prior efforts that involved using bulkheads reinforced with riprap only increased erosion. The removal of sand dunes also accelerated erosion and was eventually outlawed, along with bulkheads and riprap on beaches. Protecting dunes with sand fencing, as shown below, and by planting sea oats became sanctioned erosion stabilization methods.

These cottages were built in 1955, after Hurricane Hazel had eradicated Cherry Grove Beach's oceanfront development the previous October. The hurricane was a nightmare for property owners and insurance companies, as several insurers declared bankruptcy following Hurricane Hazel. However, building supply stores and building contractors were on a roll.

HEALTH AND HAPPINESS AT "CAMP NIXON" CHERRY GROVE BEACH.
PO OCEAN DRIVE. S. C.

Camp Nixon's family day is captured in this 1938 surf photograph. This nautical camp for boys ages 9 to 17 offered two- and four-week sessions annually, culminating with a three-day yacht cruise to Georgetown. Over 800 boys attended the 1938 camp. Founded in 1925 by director W.B. Covington, general secretary of the YMCA in Florence, South Carolina, the camp occupied 30 acres donated by Nicholas Foy Nixon.

DINING HALL, CAMP NIXON
"BY THE SEA", WAMPEE, SOUTH CAROLINA

The newly completed dining hall at Camp Nixon appears ready for hungry campers in this 1938 view, which lists its address as Wampee, South Carolina—an established community about 12 miles inland. The camp had a Wampee mailing address but was physically located in Little River Neck, overlooking Cherry Grove Beach.

The Meetin' House at Camp Nixon, shown in 1938, was the focal point of this early camp. Campers and counselors met here for group activities, including games, arts and crafts, and other programs. This camp was situated on a surviving segment of the colonial Kings Highway, which George Washington traveled during his tour of the South in 1791.

The Future Farmers of America (FFA) maintained a summer camp near Cherry Grove Beach for boys who belonged to the organization. It was situated west of Cherry Grove and accessed via Little River Neck Road. FFA Circle Drive is a street that memorializes the camp. A national student organization, FFA encourages agricultural and leadership skills.

Most of Tilghman Fishing Pier's 976 feet washed away during Hurricane Hazel in 1954, when Charles Tilghman was its contact. It had claimed to be South Carolina's newest and longest fishing pier in 1950, but it was also one of its shortest surviving piers. This pier was rebuilt, but its owners unwillingly surrendered it to the ocean during Hurricane Hugo in 1989; it was not rebuilt again.

Tilghman Beach, S. C. From the Air

A c. 1949 view of Tilghman Beach with Cherry Grove Beach in the background shows its minimal development. These were the days when fish camps operated every fall on the shores of today's North Myrtle Beach, with crews from Little River and other nearby locations coming to take advantage of this wide-open strand to operate commercial seining businesses.

This is Tilghman Beach in 1954, before it was devastated by Hurricane Hazel. Now located within the Ocean Drive section of North Myrtle Beach, this inherited property—also known as Tilghman Estates—was developed by owners Horace L. Tilghman and Charles T. Tilghman Jr. as a residential community of custom homes surrounding natural freshwater lakes. Charles Hartford Lewis served as the property's caretaker from 1922 until 1964.

The rebuilt Tilghman Fishing Pier, pictured in the 1960s, was destroyed again when Hurricane Hugo hit the area on September 22, 1989. The coincidence of Hurricanes Hazel and Hugo both beginning with the letter H is frequently noted, as they were similarly destructive storms. Hurricane Hugo was the stronger storm, with peak winds of 160 miles an hour.

Hurricane Helene damaged McElveen's Drug Store, located on Ocean Drive Beach's Main Street at Ocean Boulevard, on September 27, 1958. This was another Category 4 hurricane with peak winds of 150 miles per hour. Destroyed awnings and flooding are evident in this photograph taken from the town square on the day Helene came ashore.

Two

OCEAN DRIVE BEACH

A group of men appear in silhouette against the rising sun at Ocean Drive Beach as they prepare to launch a commercial seining net through the breaking surf. Hoping for a bountiful catch, they carefully align with the net so as to avoid tangles or gaps in their synchronized efforts to surprise schools of fish in the surf and haul them ashore before the disoriented fish can escape the net's grasp.

This postcard featuring Roberts Pavilion, as viewed from the strand in 1937, names its location as Loris, South Carolina, which is 23 miles away and was an established town long before Ocean Drive Beach became a destination. Bertha Roberts, of the nearby Green Sea community, had this pavilion built and leased it to Roy Harrelson. Following Hurricane Hazel in 1954, Harrelson purchased the newly cleared site and built a replacement pavilion, adding an amusement park to it.

Vacationing on "Carolina's Finest Strand", Ocean Drive Beach, S. C.

A wooden boardwalk leads into Roberts Pavilion as shown around 1940. Shifting sand in this wide-open beach environment frequently covered outdoor boardwalks. Pavilion guests who came to dance did not like sand in their shoes, so boardwalks were regularly swept in order to keep guests happy. The music not only kept playing, it made history.

Cars were randomly parked on the beach surrounding Roberts Pavilion in this image from late 1930s, before traffic became so congested that parking had to be organized. Most of these cars are 1930s models. However, in the years following the Great Depression, money remained tight, so cars were not often traded; therefore, some 1920s vehicles are also shown here.

A Main Street view of Roberts Pavilion at the intersection of Ocean Boulevard provides insight into the pavilion's offerings via the signage painted on its exterior walls. A Pavilion Café side entrance advertised steaks, chops, and seafood. Burgers, Schlitz beer, and Coca-Cola were also advertised as being available on the premises.

The crowds never seemed to stop coming to Roberts Pavilion in the late 1930s as the word spread about good times to be had at this beachfront pavilion in a sleepy little coastal town named Ocean Drive Beach. Bottled Coca-Colas were sold here, likely in the Pavilion Soda Shop, as advertised on the side of the building.

Roberts Pavilion, Ocean Drive, South Carolina

Not long after Roberts Pavilion opened, guests began embellishing its white exterior walls with autographs and graffiti. Most prominent is "G'boro '38," which attests to the distances from which early visitors came. Greensboro, North Carolina, is 200 miles from Ocean Drive Beach. A breezy patio with ocean views was ideal for memorable romantic evenings at this dance pavilion.

Roberts Pavilion was a success from its opening in 1936 until it was destroyed by Hurricane Hazel in 1954, as it introduced a majority of its early visitors to a world beyond their daily lives. As the music showcased at the pavilion evolved from rhythm and blues to jitterbug tunes (later renamed beach music), the guests just kept on dancing.

Separate bathhouses, with showers for men and women, at Roberts Pavilion enabled visitors to arrive early for a day of swimming and enjoying the beach followed by a shower and change into clothes suitable for an evening at the pavilion. This was ideal for guests who lived within a reasonable driving distance and could return home after the evening's fun. Signage on the back of the pavilion designated the bathhouse entrances.

Main Street at Night, Ocean Drive Beach, S. C.

Evenings on Main Street in Ocean Drive had a magical quality in the 1940s, as shown in this postcard image featuring a full moon above the ocean and, undoubtedly, the sound of breaking waves in the background. The Ocean Drive Theatre's marquee is brightly lit, and the theater was likely packed with moviegoers. Roberts Pavilion is at the end of Main Street on the right, and Griste's Drug Store is in the foreground at right.

Street Scene, Ocean Drive, S. C.

Looking up Main Street from the north side of Roberts Pavilion, Ocean Drive Beach looks empty in the daytime. Perhaps everyone is on the beach, soaking up the Carolina surf and sunshine for which its beaches are renowned. I.J. Lowman's Red and White Grocery, James Dew's Hardware, and Hardwick's Cafeteria were other businesses that would join this beach town's Main Street in the coming years.

Main Boulevard, Ocean Drive Beach, S. C.

Downtown Ocean Drive Beach businesses on the south side of Main Street included, from left to right, Roberts Pavilion, Ocean Drive Theatre, Wiley's Soda Shop and Barbeque, and Griste's Drug Store (with a post office located in its front right corner). The barbeque chef drilled a hole in the wall of his restaurant adjoining the Ocean Drive Theatre so the tempting aroma of barbeque would attract the attention of moviegoing patrons, which it did.

Main Street at Night,
Ocean Drive Beach, S. C.

Main Street in Ocean Drive came alive at night, with many of these parked cars likely belonging to out-of-towners who came to enjoy the nightlife at Roberts Pavilion and perhaps eat dinner and stay overnight at the beach. Two movie theaters on Main Street also contributed to downtown evening traffic around 1950, as shown here.

A highlight of the Amusement Center at the Ocean Drive Pavilion was its Ferris wheel. Located behind an oceanfront bathhouse, the wheel sprang into motion as vacationers departed the beach and evening settled over this cozy town. The merry-go-round and other whirling, twirling rides await their passengers. A banner behind the Ferris wheel encourages departing visitors to "Hurry Back."

An oceanfront trampoline park named the Jumping Jimminie was an immediate success beside the Ocean Drive Pavilion in the early 1960s. These in-ground trampolines were considered safer than the raised alternatives, but the park lasted only a few years before a beer joint named the Beach Party replaced it.

These girls appear to be enjoying colorful iced refreshments at the Ocean Drive Pavilion's concession stand between beach activities. Snow cones remain a quintessential summer treat during days of sun, sand, and surf. Vendors also like snow cones because of the treat's easy assembly and high profitability.

The Ocean Drive Pavilion included a bingo parlor around 1960, when Ocean Drive's population was 313, and both adults and children played bingo. "Vintage" adults still play bingo, but today's youth prefer electronic entertainment. Ocean Drive Amusements, owned by John Holcombe Jr., was a local competitor.

Putt-Putt Golf Course offered guests 18 holes of carpet golf for 35¢ per person. The course adjoined the Ocean Drive Pavilion and Amusement Center and was later replaced by the coastal-themed Jack Pot Golf. Nearby, Ocean Drive Carpet Golf was owned by James M. Gardner. Miniature golf remains a classic family entertainment all along the Grand Strand, with myriad themes represented at its innumerable courses.

In the mid-20th century, double dating was generally preferred by teenagers who were new to the dating scene because another couple helped to keep the conversation lively. Local beaches offered countless opportunities for couples. Beach strolls, movie dates, and shared ice-cream floats at a soda fountain were inexpensive dates that sometimes led to beach romances.

Ocean Drive Pavilion and Amusement Center was owned by Roy Harrelson, who leased nearby space to traveling carnivals with colorful, noisy rides that drew paying guests to his other pavilion entertainments. Harrelson later purchased used amusement rides from the Myrtle Beach Pavilion to fill his outdoor park. Dancing, bingo, bowling, roller-skating, concessions, and midway rides were all enjoyed here.

The oceanfront Grand Strand Restaurant served live Maine lobsters and choice Western beef. Vegetable dinners were a favorite entree too. However, Sunday dinners were the specialty of this restaurant owned by James E. and Doris Baldwin. Families viewed the restaurant's Sunday dinners as an opportunity to greet friends, neighbors, and other acquaintances while enjoying a day away from home cooking.

C.W. Blankenship owned The Pad, a shag-dancing, beer-drinking, good-time hangout. Sentimentality surrounding memories of this and other Ocean Drive clubs, including Duck's Night Life, eventually resulted in former beach lifeguard Gene "Swink" Laughter forming the Society of Stranders, or SOS, to host semiannual reunion weekends for all who wished to revisit their carefree youths. The reunions fill Ocean Drive with older adults who renew friendships while shag dancing.

Case's Place on Highway 17 in Ocean Drive Beach was a late-1940s gift shop owned by Dwight L. Case, who had a second store located in downtown Ocean Drive. Case had humorous postcards promoting his two gift shops, as shown here. These stores are now gone, as Case died in 1982. In his youth, he had managed a small wooden dance pavilion that predated Roberts Pavilion.

The Pad expanded by merging with Fat Harold's Beach Club, named for owner Harold Bessent, dubbed the "King of Shag." Located on Ocean Boulevard across from the pavilion, its attractions included massive crowds of young adults, a jukebox full of beach music, and extra-cold beers. Bessent was inducted into the Shaggers Hall of Fame and received additional honors for his promotional and philanthropic achievements prior to his death in 2015.

The Spanish Galleon, another popular beer joint in Ocean Drive, was started by Buddy Owens and is pictured here in the 1960s. Its pirate theme distinguished it from other jukebox bars, which collectively made Ocean Drive famous. The best-selling beers—Budweiser and Pabst Blue Ribbon—seldom varied from one juke joint to another, but the number of empty beer cans littering the premises at closing indicated the crowd's favorite hangouts.

The oceanfront Beach Party was another wildly popular hangout for socializing and shagging to beach music with a cold beer in hand. Many young people who visited the Beach Party in its heyday autographed its brick walls. This late-1960s addition to the established nightlife venues in the area helped put Ocean Drive Beach atop the dating scene throughout the Carolinas and beyond from the 1940s into the 1980s. Other renowned Carolina shag havens included the Beach Club on Highway 17 between North Myrtle and Myrtle Beaches; the Pawleys (Island) Pavilion; the Coachman and Four Club near Bennettsville, South Carolina; and the Inn at Lake Lure, North Carolina. Spring breaks yielded record crowds at Ocean Drive from the mid-1960s to the mid-1980s, which was when North Myrtle Beach clamped down on underage drinking and other violations that tended to occur during spring-break time.

The formerly expansive wooden Ocean Drive Pavilion resembled a scrap lumber pile interspersed with slabs of green shingles after Hurricane Hazel swept through on October 15, 1954. The landmark event erased most oceanfront construction while clearing a swath for modern accommodations here and all along the Grand Strand. Charming cottages from Ocean Drive's youthful beginnings were ruined overnight and eventually replaced with more sophisticated beach resorts.

Griste's Drug Store on Main Street in Ocean Drive Beach was a handsome new downtown addition when pharmacist Dr. Wiley S. Griste built it in 1945. An inclusive post office, with Dr. Griste serving as postmaster, was a bonus feature that led to the advertising slogan, "A grand drug store on the Grand Strand." The pharmacy was later sold to A.L. Wood.

McElveen's Drug Store was a Rexall-affiliated pharmacy opened by Dr. G.H. McElveen, who also sold real estate between his time filling prescriptions. McElveen's was strategically located "on the square"—Ocean Drive's principal corner where Main Street met Ocean Boulevard. Next door was Wood's 5&10¢ Store, which was later owned by A.D. Pollard, who also owned Pollard's Drug Sundry Store, in Cherry Grove Beach, with a soda fountain and beachwear merchandise.

The Beach Shop, Ocean Drive Beach, S. C.

The Beach Shop on Main Street's square at Ocean Boulevard was known for fashionable men's, women's, and children's swimwear and sportswear, along with nautical gifts and beach-related merchandise. This store maintained a huge inventory because it was a shopping destination for vacationers who lived inland but wanted the latest resort-wear clothing, which was usually available first on the coast.

The Beach Shop took a hit during Hurricane Hazel in 1954. In addition to suffering extensive damage to the downtown area, as shown here, Ocean Drive lost 450 houses. The cleanup and restoration was accomplished fairly efficiently over the winter months without beach guests present, and the 1955 spring season saw a downtown ready for business. The Toggery Shoppe, owned by Joyce and Harry E. Thomas, was another popular clothing store on Ocean Drive's Main Street.

Owned by Melvin and Mary Moore Gould, the Beach Shop was restored and had sporty new signage when it reopened in 1955. Spring merchandise that had been preordered in the prior year arrived and was used for restocking the store's inventory. A busy summer was anticipated, because Hurricane Hazel had garnered national press coverage of Ocean Drive Beach. Vacationers came to see for themselves how this popular beach was impacted.

When a beach house rests on a car, that car is totaled. When Hurricane Hazel struck in 1954, many houses floated off their oceanfront foundations; back then, buildings were not required to be attached to their foundations. Many front-row houses landed on surviving remnants of Ocean Boulevard, and others ended up farther away. Extensive debris was hazardous to the curious public, so the National Guard arrived to limit access to residents and nonresident property owners.

After Hazel, remnants of the Anchorage Apartments were found two blocks south of its original oceanfront site and on the fourth row of inland houses, where the waterborne structure had smashed into an existing house. Upon closer inspection, beneath the structure's black roof, teacups were still hanging from cup hooks in a tilted kitchen cabinet, while the cabinet's doors had been forced open by shifting stacks of plates and bowls, most of which lay broken below it.

In 1954, houses landed on Ocean Boulevard during Hurricane Hazel after the ocean's powerful surge pushed almost the entire row of oceanfront buildings inland. Some structures collapsed onto the boulevard, while others crashed into second-row houses. Home furnishings, kitchen appliances, bathroom fixtures, plumbing pipes, electrical wiring, water heaters, breaker boxes, and countless other ruined items were strewn everywhere.

Ocean Boulevard was reduced to a ravine when the seawater and excess rain from Hurricane Hazel quickly receded once the storm had passed. Reclaiming belongings was challenging, as the saltwater ruined almost everything. This was the first major challenge that young Ocean Drive Beach faced after incorporating only six years earlier, in 1948. Neighboring Crescent Beach was only a year old, and Windy Hill and Cherry Grove Beaches had not yet incorporated.

This idle wooden fishing boat on Ocean Drive Beach likely belonged to a commercial seining operation that harvested fish from the surf. Handcrafted wooden boats are scarce now, so nostalgia for these scratch-built boats is something worth celebrating. At the annual Georgetown Wooden Boat Show, held in nearby Georgetown, South Carolina, teams compete to build a wooden boat and prove its buoyancy at the riverfront while crowds cheer for their favorite boatbuilding team.

By 1958, Ocean Drive Beach's downtown appeared as if it had never been uprooted, but a closer look at the oceanfront reveals that most prime real estate remained sparsely redeveloped. In 1954, local law enforcement, led by police chief Merlin Bellamy, effectively handled Hurricane Hazel as they undertook tasks that ranged from notifying residents about evacuating to helping people who needed assistance to keeping peace and order in the aftermath of the hurricane.

56

A 1958 bird's-eye view of the Ocean Drive Pavilion taken from offshore reveals that it included a miniature golf course with a 19th-hole beer pavilion, a bathhouse with float and umbrella rentals, a merry-go-round, a Ferris wheel, several rides for young children, a large pavilion offering bingo, and a grill restaurant. There is no pavilion parking except in the "horseshoe" where Main Street terminates at the oceanfront and within the street's wide median.

The Justamere Guest House, shown around 1960, was a second-row Ocean Boulevard property located two blocks from downtown Ocean Drive Beach. It offered rooms, apartments, and cottage rentals described as "home-like." Mr. and Mrs. A.G. Greene were its owner-managers. The guesthouse's management suggested: "Relax at the seashore."

"Excellent" perfectly describes the summer season depicted in this late-1960s aerial view of downtown Ocean Drive Beach. Cars are parked everywhere and spilling into Main Street, while beachgoers appear as polka dots across the strand and in the surf too. Downtown merchants were likely in a great mood, as were their many beach guests from the Carolinas and beyond.

Hoskins Restaurant was opened in 1948 by Hubert and Leona Hoskins and later owned by Bryan and Joan Floyd. The fried seafood platter remains the most requested menu item as this restaurant approaches 75 years of continuous operation—that is a lot of waitstaff serving piping-hot seafood platters nightly for decades! A line forms daily at the front door for lunch and dinner.

The USS *Sequoia*, the presidential yacht, was docked in Ocean Drive Beach from 1978 to 1980. After serving 11 US presidents for recreational purposes, it was open for tours at Vereen's Marina near the Ocean Drive Beach entrance, where it entertained curiosity seekers and history buffs for two years. The William H. Hussey family, of Ocean Drive Beach, led the local acquisition of the yacht. Two years after the acquisition, the yacht was resold and slated for an overhaul to restore it to its original glory. This picture of the yacht was taken in 1925.

This c. 1960 offshore aerial view of Ocean Drive Beach's downtown shows a simpler business district than the one at the top of the previous page from a decade later. Two oceanfront miniature golf courses had not yet been built, and the oceanfront trampoline park is occupying the site where the Beach Party would soon be constructed. Each year between 1960 to 1970 brought changes to Ocean Drive when tourism was beginning to explode on the Grand Strand.

CATALINA GUEST HOUSE

OCEAN DRIVE BEACH, S. C.

Catalina Guest House was a second-row property with ocean-view rooms located 75 yards from the strand. It served three meals each day and offered private or connecting baths. A homelike atmosphere was provided by its owners, Mr. and Mrs. J.C. Turner. Many second-row beach houses were updated for room rentals and meal service by adding or reconfiguring spaces to accommodate guests in addition to the family already residing there.

Hauling a sturdy net through the surf and onto shore yielded mullet, spots, and various other fish. A small boat positioned the net offshore. Lead weights on one length of the net anchored it to the ocean floor, while cork floats on the net's opposing length held it at the ocean's surface. Some members of the crew gripped staffs at each end of the net, while other crew members stood in between to entrap fish by advancing the net ashore while maintaining its perimeters.

60

Crowds often gathered when a seining net was pulled through the surf—they were there as much for the novelty of the experience as for the opportunity to purchase fresh fish. Prices for these fish were the lowest available, and the freshness of the fish was at its peak. Seining crews sometimes cleaned and cooked part of their catch at temporary nearby fish camps, then dined on fried fish and sold the leftovers to hungry observers.

The Buccaneer Motel Apartments at 401 South Ocean Boulevard were open year-round. This oceanfront accommodation, pictured here in 1964 and managed in the early 1970s by H. Tom Roberts of Bessent and Roberts Realty, was two blocks south of Ocean Drive Beach's Main Street. In 1972, room rates ranged from $18 daily for a room that slept two to $30 daily for a two-room apartment that could sleep six.

The Surf Golf and Beach Club on Highway 17 in Ocean Drive Beach opened in 1960 on 200 wooded acres with 18 golf holes and 27 lakes. Ed Bullock of Winston-Salem, North Carolina, was the Surf's first golf professional. Green fees were $4 with a guest card and $5.50 otherwise. Fees steadily increased as golf clubs competed to be the finest facilities, while bag push carts and caddies yielded to four-seater golf carts used for navigating the course.

The Sea Sound Motel was on South Ocean Boulevard at Third Avenue, two blocks from the pavilion. It overlooked the ocean, meaning it was a second-row property. The owner-manager was John Ormsby, followed by Charles and Montie Johnson. By 1967, this motel had been extensively renovated and added a pancake house offering full breakfasts and snacks throughout the day.

Jackson Villa was a second-row guesthouse that served home-cooked meals three times daily. James Blakeney Jackson owned this property. He also served on the Ocean Drive Beach town council and owned Jackson Realtors and Insurers, offering real estate sales and rentals as well as insurance. Billie Jackson, James's wife, was the villa's hostess because her husband (and, later, her son) was busy brokering deals.

An aerial view of the Surf Golf and Beach Club highlights its wooded surroundings and proximity to the coast. Other North Myrtle Beach golf clubs that opened in the 1960s included Possum Trot, Beachwood, and Robber's Roost (in 1968) and Azalea Sands and Eagle Nest (in 1969). Possum Trot is the only one of these pioneer North Myrtle Beach courses that is no longer in operation.

In 1940, Ocean Drive Hotel was a three-story wooden oceanfront hotel (pictured above) with exposed rafter tails and a wraparound porch perfect for capturing ocean breezes. It was described modestly as "a comfortable place where you may spend your vacation and enjoy it." All of this ended in 1954 after Hurricane Hazel struck, resulting in a replacement motel. A new Ocean Drive Motel (below), constructed after Hazel, was a lower, longer structure built of concrete block and faced with a stone veneer on its ground floor. This new building, renamed as a "motel," retained a favorite amenity—a beachfront patio for socializing amid its coastal atmosphere. W.C. "Bill" Lyerly Jr. was the motel's owner and manager.

Ocean Drive Beach was the setting for this 1953 photograph featuring three children learning to build sandcastles. As vacationers in the nearby Anchorage Apartments, they were enjoying themselves, coated in fine beach sand from their heads to their toes. Following a quick dip in the ocean, they were refreshed and resumed their sandcastle construction.

Tourism was booming when a third version of the Ocean Drive Motel emerged in the 1960s with an oceanfront three-story building and a two-story annex behind it. This motel featured a "sparkling" Olympic-size swimming pool, "handsome" rooms, "luxurious" efficiencies, and "deluxe" suites. The enthusiastic owners further described their motel as "a year round vacation wonderland."

THE CAROLINA QUEEN Operates From Three Locations:
SUMMER . . . Vereen's Marina, U. S. 17, Ocean Drive, South Carolina
FALL . . . . Ocean Plaza Pier, Myrtle Beach, South Carolina
WINTER . . . Gateway Docks, Sunrise Avenue, Ft. Lauderdale, Florida

The *Carolina Queen* pleasure and fishing craft docked every summer at Vereen's Marina, which was near the intersection of Highway 17 and Ocean Drive and convenient to vacationers. The 83-foot craft with twin diesel engines had a 90-person capacity and drew crowds wanting to experience deep-sea fishing or perhaps cruise the coastline in hopes of sighting porpoises and other sea creatures. This fully equipped boat was also available for charter.

The oceanfront Bel-Aire Motel, located at 102 North Ocean Boulevard, was owned by Herbert G. Myers and Robert R. Snyder. Betty Jean Myers assisted in its operation. This U-shaped motel with an interior courtyard was originally naturally cooled by cross ventilation, with television viewing available in the lobby. Subsequent owner couples included the Lloyd Bells, the Roscoe Bells, the David Beardmores, and the Ed Grices. By 1991, the Bel-Aire had 73 units.

TARHEEL INN

OCEAN DRIVE BEACH, S. C.

The Tarheel Inn belonged to a North Carolinian, Ovaline T. Bridgers, of nearby Fair Bluff. Ocean Drive Beach has always been popular with North Carolina vacationers because this northeastern corner of South Carolina borders the Tarheel State. Many early settlers in the once-remote area had ancestors who arrived in the country at the Bay of Albemarle and settled across the region before Carolina was split into two states.

The Nor-Bet Apartments at 1009 South Ocean Boulevard belonged to Norwood and Betty Gasque. Norwood was the town attorney of Latta, South Carolina, and a family court judge with a distinguished career; a Dillon County highway bridge is named for him. The Nor-Bet had four two-bedroom units that slept two to nine people and several one-bedroom efficiencies that slept five to six people. Air-conditioning helped with everyone vacationing together!

An Ocean Drive "hanging moon" was an affordable souvenir widely replicated in the 1940s. These teenagers from McClellanville, South Carolina, are Phillis Barrett (now McGrew), at left, and Emily Morrison (now Baldwin). Their 1946 visit to Ocean Drive Beach is preserved for posterity, as this image now belongs to the Village Museum in McClellanville, where these childhood friends worked together in their retirement as museum volunteers.

The oceanfront Helms Motel and Apartments were owned and operated in the 1950s by James Marvin Helms and his wife, Leona Eason Helms. A decade later, Ruby H. Allison was the owner-manager of this 304 North Ocean Boulevard property located only four blocks from the Ocean Drive Pavilion. By 1982, Dean and Gail DeMattio owned the 35 units at the Helms.

The Sea Shell Motel was a second-row property located at 305 North Ocean Boulevard and owned and managed in the 1960s by Mr. and Mrs. H.A. Brady. In the 1980s, Mrs. H.B. Buffkin Jr. was associated with this motel; at that time, it closed for five months each winter.

Crescent Beach Court, later renamed Crescent Motor Court, was owned and operated by Evelyn Bellamy Long. She was a sister of Roscoe Bellamy, owner of Roscoe's Seafood Market in Cherry Grove Beach, and police chief Merlin Bellamy in Ocean Drive Beach. Whether Evelyn Long needed fresh fish to cook for dinner or crisis assistance at her Highway 17 motor court, she knew who to call!

The oceanfront Lucy Villa in Ocean Drive consisted of four apartments claimed to be "the most fashionable accommodations available" in the early 1950s. They belonged to Lucy Lewis of Florence, South Carolina, and were further described as being large and strictly private. The main two-story building faced the oceanfront, and a smaller structure was beside the boulevard.

Owner, Lucy Lewis
1019 Cherokee — Phone 8352
Florence, S. C.

By 1960, the Sea Vista Motel, shown in a picture taken from the second floor of the horseshoe-shaped lodging, offered oceanfront apartments and a pool. Owned and managed by Mr. and Mrs. V.C. Arnette, it was located at 300 North Ocean Boulevard. Joseph J. and Frances E. McMillan later owned its one-, two-, and three-bedroom apartments. Its sand dunes were eventually restored, and a row of distinctive, round penthouses were added atop its two stories.

The Coquina Terrace
Ocean Drive Beach, S. C.

The Coquina Terrace, built around 1950, claimed to be the Grand Strand's first oceanfront motel, meaning that its 20 rooms offered direct outside access with parking nearby. As prosperity grew following World War II, motels eclipsed hotels as preferred family accommodations. This motel was among the finest for its time, with each room having a private bath.

The oceanfront Grand Motel at 106 North Ocean Boulevard was managed by Barbara and Jerome Walker in the early 1970s. Earlier, Charles and Sherry Sendler were its owner-managers. It had efficiency apartments and rooms with so many perks that one might assume grand times were had by all at the Grand Motel. However, when Hurricane Hugo struck in 1989, the Grand Motel vanished into the ocean.

Five reasons to be a beach lifeguard are shown in this Ocean Drive Beach photograph. Lifeguards ruled the beaches—a fairly easy task when their kingdom consisted of happy, relaxed beachgoers. However, monitoring ocean swimmers amid countless beach distractions was a heavy responsibility for young adults, especially first-time lifeguards. Girls on the beach could not resist flirting with the handsome, bronzed lifeguards, and they usually returned the compliments.

The Mar-Vista Motel at 605 South Ocean Boulevard offered a pool with a waterslide, in-room telephones, color cable television, cots upon request, linens, refrigerators, daily maid service, and more. This three-story oceanfront motel reflected a trend of building taller motels as the beaches became crowded and additional land became unavailable. Libby and Richard Nixon were the contacts for Mar-Vista's 43 units. A rebuilt Mar Vista (minus the hyphen) remains in business.

The Tryon Seville Resort Motel, pictured in 1966, was located at 1321 South Ocean Boulevard. Trudy and John Jessup and later Wallace Best were associated with this motel in the early 1970s. This large, esteemed motel had expanded to 75 units, including a penthouse, by the early 1980s. Golf packages combining motel rooms and green fees at a reduced rate were highly successful here.

HOTEL DOUGLAS MacARTHUR

MRS. V. C. ARNETTE, Owner and Mgr. — OCEAN DRIVE, S. C.   5B-H369

The three-story Hotel Douglas MacArthur was built in the mid-1940s at Ocean Drive Beach. It was on oceanfront property but set back from the beach with a deep front lawn facing the ocean. Mrs. V.C. Arnette was its owner and manager. Hurricane Hazel destroyed this young hotel in 1954.

This stately church was founded on April 25, 1947, as the Presbyterian Church at Ocean Drive Beach and later renamed the Ocean Drive Presbyterian Church. The Perrin and McLean families donated adjoining properties at Sixth Avenue South, which were elevated to minimize the potential for flooding at the church. As the church grew, a new sanctuary, shown here, was completed in 1989 to adjoin its predecessor, and the congregation now has 800 members.

Setting the table was a shared responsibility amongst the Junior Homemakers of America when its members converged on Ocean Drive Beach for summer camp around 1951. Built in the 1940s, the camp was near Ocean Drive Presbyterian Church. The camp director was Kathryn Wright from Sumter, South Carolina, and the campers were from South Carolina schools within a five-county area.

Junior Homemakers of America campers are shown enjoying a beach day around 1960. The group's nearby 10-acre camp consisted of at least six dormitories accommodating up to 500 people, so every camp day likely included groups of campers spending time on the nearby Ocean Drive Beach.

Mess Hall, Junior Homemakers Camp, Ocean Drive, S. C.

There was a warm atmosphere at the Junior Homemakers of America camp, and its central building was this dining and activity facility constructed in the 1940s. One camper mailed this brief message home to her parents in 1948: "In spite of my forebodings, camp is fine. We had a grand boat ride this afternoon and go to Myrtle Beach tomorrow. Miss you though!"

The dining and assembly hall at the Junior Homemakers of America camp presented a welcoming scene around 1960, with colorful flower arrangements on every table. A marble tablet mounted above the fireplace reads, "Ocean Drive Junior Homemakers Camp dedicated to Lillian Clare Hoffman, true friend and wise counselor."

Junior Homemakers of America campers enjoyed the surf at Ocean Drive Beach in the early 1950s. Other camp highlights included Wednesday night cookouts hosted by the Future Farmers of America campers in nearby Little River Neck and Thursday night square dances hosted by the Junior Homemakers of America campers with the Future Farmers of America campers as their invited guests.

This excursion tour aboard the *Martha Ann* in nearby waters must have been a highlight for the Junior Homemakers of America campers. The diesel-powered wooden boat was outfitted for deep-sea fishing with Capt. J.T. Stevens and left daily at 8:00 a.m. out of nearby Little River. However, on this day around 1951, it was fully loaded with happy campers.

Adult counselors and their campers are shown relaxing in front of their dining and assembly hall in this view of the Ocean Drive Junior Homemakers Camp. Campers arrived in school buses from their hometowns, where they belonged to Junior Homemakers of America clubs in their respective schools. Regular club meetings throughout the school year instructed the girls in home management and related topics.

Drip sandcastles provided hours of fairy-tale construction as the sun and surf slowly eroded a castle's fragile architecture, necessitating renovations. Upgrades and additions were always options, or perhaps a rising tide necessitated relocation, much like with real beach properties following a storm. The drip architecture of these castles involves creating a soupy mixture of sand and water to attain a consistency suitable for elaborate turrets, as shown here. These castle-building activities provide precious family interaction and create memories worthy of family pictures. This vintage sandcastle image illustrates North Myrtle Beach's extreme width at low tide, which further enhances its recreational usage.

Three

CRESCENT BEACH

In this 1970s view of Crescent Beach facing north, the town looks prosperous yet cozy. Prior to development, this beach was called the Ward Estate. The hotel beside the Crescent Beach Fishing Pier is the Holiday Inn North—one of the first national chain hotels to join the Grand Strand after Hurricane Hazel destroyed its oceanfront mom-and-pop accommodations. Crescent Beach lost 200 homes to Hazel in 1954, and additional homes were severely damaged.

Crescent Beach had a spacious downtown around 1960, with many lots available for new retail businesses. Jordan Realty Co., with Elbert Jordan at the helm, and Crescent Realty, a few doors down, were both ready for sales at their prominent locations in the downtown's main block.

The Crescent Beach Fishing Pier sold bait shrimp and minnows, rented and sold fishing tackle, and promoted their full-menu restaurant that specialized in seafood. It also promoted the 1960 Grand Strand Fishing Rodeo, an annual Greater Myrtle Beach Chamber of Commerce event with a $6,000 purse, which "reeled in" business as the pier filled with optimistic anglers.

Crescent Beach's amusement center was a focal point of its downtown. A Ferris wheel, merry-go-round, and several rides for young children were all located beside the Crescent Beach Pavilion, which was operated by R.A. Siceloff in the 1960s.

A skating rink within the Crescent Beach Pavilion and beside its amusement rides was a boost to this active town. A snack bar, café, and bingo tables completed the pavilion, offering families something to please everyone.

The three-story oceanfront Francis Noble Apartments were owned and operated by Noble Jackson and Frances Nellie Fisher Whisenant of Charlotte, North Carolina. Each of these efficiency apartments slept from four to eight people in air-conditioned comfort. This is a 1967 view of the building.

Looking north from the Royal Palms Motor Inn (visible in the left foreground of this 1980s view), one can see the natural curvature for which Crescent Beach was named. The Royal Palms, previously called the Ocean Strand Motor Inn, had 54 units that were managed by H.B. Buffkin Jr. and included a restaurant. As shown here, the inn needed some palm trees to validate its tropical name, and management soon added them.

Wilson's Candy Shoppe on Highway 17 at Crescent Beach was also home to a Gulf gas station that sold pecan pies, orange juice, Kodak film, baskets, souvenirs, beach bags, sport caps, shelled jewelry, ice cream, toys, and postcards. Owned by Mr. and Mrs. William T. Wilson Jr., the business provided patio seating near its entrance for guests to relax.

The Dixie Motel, shown in the 1960s at 2712 South Ocean Boulevard, was owned and operated by D.C. Freeman. This motel with rooms, apartments, a swimming pool, and golf privileges was a second-row property overlooking the ocean.

The exterior of Rose Gift Shop was the color of a fuchsia-pink rose, but the store was likely named for its owner, Rose H. Hooks. Located opposite Crescent Beach City Hall, it sold African violets, hammocks, jewelry, greeting cards, and "thousands of gifts and souvenirs." There was also a snack bar amid the "gifts of distinction."

The Marion Earl Apartments, shown prior to 1967, became simply the Marion Earl, an oceanfront resort motel, by the early 1970s. Married couple Marion Earl Clark and Mary Caton Clark were the owner-managers of this property at 324 Ocean Boulevard, which was later enlarged and added a swimming pool.

Cap's Cabin belonged to Capt. W.R. Whilden, a 40-year veteran of the US Merchant Marine who rented each floor as a separate apartment, beginning with the house on the left in the 1960s. Whilden later added the house on the right in the 1970s, retaining its first floor as a manager unit. These three oceanfront rental apartments had three bedrooms apiece and offered laundry access for a "nominal fee," but no charge for the patriotic flag display. Each unit was $175 weekly.

Trinity Methodist Church in Crescent Beach began in September 1946 as Ocean View Chapel Methodist Church. Its 11 charter members had the surnames Lamb, Baldwin, and Jordan, and the church's first pastor was Rev. R. Newton Wells, who was succeeded by Rev. Carl L. Parker. Within a year, the small congregation had secured four lots for a church, constructed the building, and dedicated it. By 1957, their membership had grown to 175 members, and the church needed a larger sanctuary, which was built in 1958.

Hotel Ocean Strand, Crescent Beach, Ocean Drive, South Carolina

The three-story Hotel Ocean Strand, shown in 1944, was managed by C.J. Gasque. It provided guests with free access to badminton, archery, shuffleboard courts, horseshoes, and other sports. Management also mentioned that the beach was "unexcelled for driving, racing, and bathing."

Hotel Ocean Strand's three stories appeared to be sinking following Hurricane Hazel in 1954. This graphic representation of Hazel's impact was photographed from all angles before the building was demolished. The hotel, which is shown intact above, is pictured here from Ocean Boulevard, where only its section closest to the boulevard remains recognizable.

Hurricane Hazel's impact surrounding the Hotel Ocean Strand, which is in the lower left foreground of this image, was colossal. Former oceanfront homes and guest accommodations were pushed back from their original sites and found either resting on Ocean Boulevard or against second-row houses, some of which were also damaged by floating structures. Other former oceanfront structures were missing, which accounted for the shattered building materials strewn everywhere.

After Hurricane Hazel, the Hotel Ocean Strand was replaced with an updated Ocean Strand Motel, which was later renamed the Ocean Strand Motor Inn. Located on Ocean Boulevard at Seventeenth Avenue South, it was managed by Mary and Robert Clyde McCord. David Seitz and Mrs. Fleming Jensen were managers associated with this property after it became a motor inn.

Seine Fishing, Crescent Beach, S. C.

"America's Finest Strand"

Commercial seining occurred at Crescent Beach and all along the Grand Strand at one time or another. It was prominent during the first half of the 20th century and into the 1950s, which was when crews gradually shifted northward, retreating from tourism development. Business expenses were minimal—a sturdy wooden boat, an elongated haul net, wooden transport boxes, a truck to deliver the catch to market, and a reliable workforce.

The Royal Palms Motor Inn and Restaurant was described by management as "an oceanfront resort motel located on the world's widest strand." Its one- and two-bedroom apartments at the intersection of Ocean Boulevard and Lyon Street featured cable television. This property was previously the Hotel Ocean Strand (shown on pages 86 and 87).

The Sea Crest Guest House was a second-row property located slightly north of the Hotel Ocean Strand. Food and cleanliness were the management's priorities for this three-and-a-half-story guesthouse, shown above around 1950. It was later sold to Mr. and Mrs. David Carmichael, who renamed it the Crescent Lodge and bought new signage for it, as shown below. The Carmichaels opened the lodge year-round while continuing its dining room service. This guesthouse of rooms and efficiency apartments was later sold to Mr. and Mrs. W.D. Skipper, who continued its operation. It survived Hurricane Hazel despite another house landing at its front door.

Houser Cottage was a second-row rental property located at 119 Ocean Boulevard in Crescent Beach. In 1974, its upstairs apartment had three bedrooms and slept 10 people for $160 weekly, and its downstairs apartment had one bedroom but slept six people for $85 weekly. With all 16 guests present, this was quite a full Houser! The rentals were handled by White Realty Company, led by Royce White.

Ocean Breeze Motor Court, U. S. #17, Crescent Beach, S. C.
F. M. Scurry, Mgr.

Ocean Breeze Motor Court and Restaurant on Highway 17 was managed by F.M. Scurry and Bill Lempesis around 1950, when its restaurant was known for Greek salads; steaks, chicken, and seafood were also available. The motor court's advertising suggested its rooms were beautiful, modern, and fireproof. The latter term usually meant the rooms were built of concrete blocks.

Piedmont, Southern, and Inland Airlines offered flight service via the Myrtle Beach Municipal Airport in the Crescent Beach section of North Myrtle Beach. Built during World War II, this mile-long landing strip with an asphalt tarmac was first named Wampee Flight Strip. It was the principal airfield for Myrtle Beach air traffic from 1956 to 1976, when Myrtle Beach Air Force Base began leasing its airport facilities. Now Grand Strand Airport, it serves general aviation needs.

The Crescent Hotel appears to be built upon the strand on this 1953 postcard. It promised "modern rates" and that it was a place "where strangers make friends." Every room had a private bath, and the food was described as excellent.

Stuckey's Pecan Shoppe on Highway 17 encouraged passing motorists to "stop, refuel, refresh." In addition to Phillips 66 gas pumps, J.B. Smith's business offered a snack bar, clean restrooms, and Stuckey's "world famous pecan log rolls" consisting of a nougat core rolled in chopped pecans. They were delicious!

This 1960s aerial view of Crescent Beach facing north shows Ocean Boulevard as one of its two paved streets. Main Street was also paved in this orderly coastal town. By 1970, the total population of North Myrtle Beach was 1,957. Summer populations within the same area are exponentially larger than its year-round population.

Pope's Motel and Restaurant on Highway 17 at Holly Street was the largest motel in Crescent Beach when it was built around 1960. It belonged to Pope and Rosa Hamilton in 1962. This motel had an oasis of shade trees at its front entrance as well as tables and chairs and a soft-drink machine nearby, all of which invited guests to sit and sip.

Zane's Grill was built and operated in the early 1950s by Lucille and W. Zane Morgan. The restaurant's specialties were barbeque smoked on premises, southern-fried chicken, steaks, chops, seafood, and lots of sandwiches. This grill restaurant was later sold and renamed the Hitching Post, which was open all night during summer and operated by Minnie and Bill Strickland.

DickManor, Crescent Beach, South Carolina

Dick Manor, built in the 1930s and shown around 1937, was a three-story oceanfront accommodation offering weekly family rates. It belonged to H.J. Dickman and included a shuffleboard court. It was such an early beach accommodation that no other buildings are visible nearby.

Crescent Beach & Ocean Drive Beach along the Grand Strand, S. C.   4

Crescent Beach is in the foreground of this c. 1950 view, and Ocean Drive Beach is in the background. The image's dominant features include Ocean Boulevard extending until it vanishes into the horizon, oceanfront structures beside the boulevard, and the fishing pier and water tower at Ocean Drive. All of this would be scrambled in just a few years later, when Hurricane Hazel arrived in 1954 and renovated the north strand area.

This is a seagull's view of Crescent Beach, facing north. Scattered beachgoers suggest this picture was likely taken during a shoulder season, when the population was below summer averages. Local residents considered fall and spring their "secret" seasons and looked forward to enjoying the beach's milder temperatures before and after a long hot summer. However, visitors eventually began extending the season, and now they come throughout the year.

Dick Manor Guest House, shown here around 1950, promoted its access to deep-sea, river, and pier fishing; surf bathing; golf; and tennis. Thankfully, management placed comfy chairs outside for less athletically inclined guests to relax during their beach vacations.

The oceanfront Sea Chateau consisted of 12 two-room apartments owned by Mr. and Mrs. J.G. Huggins. These modern—for the 1970s—units had floors of terrazzo and wall-to-wall carpet, full-size kitchen appliances, televisions, telephones, and vacuum cleaners for $150 weekly in summer. White Realty and Strand Realty were agents for this motel at different times.

Beachwood Golf Club, located beside the Grand Strand Airport west of Highway 17, has a Crescent Beach address. Eddie Steere was Beachwood's golf pro when it opened in 1968. It was designed by golf-course architect Gene Hamm, who also designed the Azalea Sands and Raccoon Run golf

On the links at Beachwood Golf Club, golfers enjoy a championship layout with 18 holes. Taken in its entirety, the Grand Strand is the "Seaside Golf Capital of the World," according to the late Jimmy D'Angelo, the original golf pro for the Dunes Golf and Beach Club in Myrtle Beach. D'Angelo was renowned as a tireless and outstanding golf promoter, for which he was nicknamed "Mr. Myrtle Beach Golf."

Beachwood Golf Club

courses in North Myrtle Beach during the 1960s. Later, J. Blakeney Jackson Jr. was a managing partner in its operation. These four photographs show Beachwood Golf Course in its early years.

The beach is what ultimately makes a Grand Strand vacation special. This party of young people was enjoying their version of beach soccer in the summer of 1961. Volleyball is another team sport often played on the wide strand at Crescent and other nearby beaches. Finding enough players for a pickup game among beachgoers is seldom a problem.

Anchorage Motel and Dining Room on Highway 17 at Crescent Beach was owned and operated by Mr. and Mrs. Al Lewis. It was located two blocks from the ocean at the highway's intersection with Lyon Road. All 20 units featured steam heat and private baths. "The utmost in comfort and good food," was its claim. The separate dining building was later replaced with a swimming pool.

By the Sea began as a three-story oceanfront apartment and guest-room accommodation that included a smaller two-story annex on the second row with additional apartments. Some units were air-conditioned, and others had electric fans. When this motel needed updating, it received renovations and a refreshed name. Owners Gene and Edith Orndoff rebranded the By the Sea Apartments and Guest Rooms as By the Sea Motel and Apartments in the 1960s. These structures at 118 South Ocean Boulevard previously included a second-row two-story building with additional apartments. As of this writing, By the Sea Motel and Apartments remains in business.

Spencer Court and Grill on Highway 17 was one of several vintage roadside motor courts built in the 1940s at Crescent Beach. Phil R. Mather and Bud S. Henderson were its resident-owners and likely also prepared its fine food served from the grill. The Spencer had 20 rooms with private baths.

The Ocean Sands Motor Inn, located at 1525 South Ocean Boulevard, was owned by Dr. George D. Gaddy and managed by David Spires in the early 1980s. Bob Eyerly was a previous resident-manager. This 36-unit high-rise hotel featured a three-bedroom penthouse. It closed each winter for three months.

The Carolina Coast Apartments, managed by Chandler Bell, were "ultra modern" when they were built in the 1960s. This oceanfront property in Crescent Beach was an L-shaped brick building well suited for families, as its apartments each held up to six people.

Crescent Beach was a busy vacation destination, as is apparent in this 1958 beach view. This may have been a Fourth of July crowd, as beach umbrellas are everywhere, and the lifeguard is seated amid the beach activity in his elevated chair with a beach umbrella too.

The oceanfront Crescent Beach Village Motel at 1801 South Ocean Boulevard had 18 units by 1991. June N. Cochrane and Vinie Carroll were two of its managers over the years.

An aerial look at the Holiday Inn North at the southern end of Crescent Beach shows the terminus of Ocean Boulevard at Thirty-seventh Avenue South, where traffic was redirected to Highway 17. This Holiday Inns of America franchise hotel regularly hosted live concerts in the 1970s featuring beach music bands, including the Tams and the Drifters, in its lounge. William W. "Bill" Wallace and Billie Sherengos were two of its innkeepers through the years, but the hotel is now gone.

An offshore view of the Holiday Inn North illustrates its impressive width and ocean frontage. A lengthy bulkhead protected this hotel, which was built almost at the water's edge during normal tides. The Crescent Beach Fishing Pier is shown at right in this image.

White Sails Motor Court had a semicircular row of individual cottages surrounding a Shell gas station and an attached dining room that was known for its fried chicken dinners. Located on Highway 17, White Sails was a classic 1940s roadside motor court. Similar early accommodations have almost disappeared from the highways today.

A young boy searches for seashell treasures on Windy Hill Beach in this picture taken around 1977. Nearby are shallow tidal pools created by wave action and containing microcosms of the ocean waiting to be explored. At varying times, these naturally occurring pools yielded seashells, starfish, fossilized sharks' teeth, sand dollars, and perhaps minnows or tiny Atlantic blue crabs—to the delight of those who searched them closely. Beachgoers sometimes call them "kiddie pools," as children especially delight in their natural gifts.

Four

WINDY HILL BEACH

"Fishing is really fabulous from Windy Hill Fishing Pier," claims a vintage postcard from the 1960s—and this was true. The Windy Hill Development Corporation that organized to buy the land and develop Windy Hill Beach also built this pier, which undoubtedly attracted buyers for nearby lots in the new town of Windy Hill.

Main Street in Windy Hill Beach looks calm on this day around 1958, but on October 15, 1954, the town lost 120 of its 270 houses and numerous businesses during Hurricane Hazel. On the right of the pier is a variety store, and on the left is an amusement pavilion.

The Covington Apartments on Pier Street at Windy Hill Fishing Pier, shown here in 1962, belonged to managers Alice and W.C. "Buck" Covington. Buck also ran Covington Realty Company in Windy Hill Beach.

Bay Court, Windy Hill Beach, South Carolina

The vintage Bay Court at Windy Hill had been operated by J.B. Hatley since 1950 with daily and weekly rates. Hatley offered additional discounts in the fall and spring, and he also managed the nearby Windy Hill Fishing Pier.

Windy Hill Fishing Pier, shown in this aerial photograph from offshore, was owned by A.J. Horton and managed by J.B. Hatley around 1950. It had a new pier patio at that time that offered meals, snacks, and sandwiches. "Open early–close late" was its slogan, which undoubtedly pleased anglers trying to squeeze in some fishing between working a day job and going home. Thomas L. Harrell was a later contact for this pier.

Windy Hill Fishing Pier

A packed north side of the Windy Hill Fishing Pier indicated fish were biting heavily in this 1965 photograph. This pier at the end of the town's main street was over 1,000 feet long before hurricanes began trimming it. The pier included a restaurant and tackle shop and claimed to be "where the big ones are always caught." Sadly, it no longer exists.

The signage for Christy's Restaurant featured a champagne glass replacing the Y in its name, suggesting festive times. Located on Highway 17 at Windy Hill Beach, Christy's offered fine dining, a full bar, and a parquet dance floor with live entertainment, all of which pleased vacationers and locals seeking to splurge on a dinner celebration enlivened with music and dancing.

The Pier View Motel overlooked Windy Hill Fishing Pier, as shown in this 1976 image. Howard and Carolyn Farris owned and operated this three-story efficiency apartment motel at 403 Thirty-seventh Avenue South in Windy Hill. An attached real estate sales office with a newspaper rack at its entrance completes this image.

Whether one prefers swinging a golf club, casting a fishing rod, or swimming in seawater, Windy Hill Beach can supply vacationers' preferences. By 1973, nearby golf courses with a North Myrtle Beach address included the Surf Golf and Beach Club, Robbers Roost Golf Club, Beachwood Golf Club, Eagle Nest Golf Club, and Azalea Sands Golf Club. Surprisingly, this was only the beginning of the Grand Strand's golf obsession.

These three artist friends packed their paints, canvases, and easels when visiting Windy Hill from West Virginia in 1982. Sheltering from the sun in a quaint gazebo built over a primary sand dune years earlier, they created memories while painting enduring images. Beach gazebos are picturesque shelters, so hopefully, this charming, weathered structure was preserved in one of their paintings.

Eyerly's Oceanfront Motel and World Famous Restaurant, built around 1945, is shown here in 1961. Robert M. "Bob" and Winnie Ruth Eyerly were its original owner-operators. A decade later, W.D. Meeks was associated with this property. Eyerly's Restaurant served three meals daily to

In 1967, the San Juan Motel was a new second-row motel offering rooms and efficiency apartments. It faced Ocean Boulevard and claimed to be "ultra modern" when wall-to-wall carpet, television, and air-conditioning were guest priorities. The San Juan Motel was advertised as being near a "famous restaurant," meaning Eyerly's (shown below).

motel guests and also served the public. With seating for 180, the restaurant welcomed all who came to enjoy fine dining with broad ocean viewing.

KIT'S FISHING PIER

"It's always yesterday at Kit's Fishing Pier" was the "hook" used to encourage fishing from this pier situated adjacent to Sherwood Forest and Ponderosa family campgrounds. This offshore aerial view shows Kit's Fishing Pier with its restaurant and arcade on the south end of Windy Hill Beach.

Kit's Fishing Pier manager Tommy Thompson built a nearby apartment motel for the convenience of avid anglers. Each unit had a pier view, so guests could determine if the fish were biting without leaving their apartment by simply counting the cars in the pier's parking lot—this was a surprisingly accurate fish indicator. Fall was the peak fishing season, and spring held second place.

The Shorecrest Motel, advertised as "oceanfront at Kit's Fishing Pier," expanded by acquiring property at 4708 Ocean Boulevard, and it eventually consisted of 92 room and efficiency apartment units. Owner-managers of the Shorecrest included C. Houston Bush, Roy Thomas, and (later) Herman Hull.

Fish were definitely biting on the day this picture was taken on the north side of Kit's Fishing Pier, which did not please casual anglers who arrived late and could not find a space. Sadly, fishing from the opposite side was hardly worth the effort. Schools of fish migrated south, and they could not resist a solid row of baited hooks suspended underwater all along the north side of the pier.

The El Mar Apartments at 4000 Ocean Boulevard, in the Windy Hill section, are shown around 1970, when Kathryn McBride was the manager. This second-row lodging was one block from the Windy Hill Fishing Pier. Abundant coco palms and palmetto trees gave these apartments an inviting tropical look, but sadly, there was no swimming pool.

Coastal Candle Makers on Highway 17 in the Windy Hill section of North Myrtle Beach capitalized on the 1970s candle craze to market a specialty item that was a necessity during earlier centuries but is now considered a decor accessory. Candles were hand-dipped on-site in various colors and sizes with multiple scented oils available to add market appeal. Business was brisk.

Thelma and Aubrey Elliott owned the Carriage House Apartments on Ocean Boulevard at Windy Hill Beach. A restaurant was later added to this second-row property. "The finest place we know of for your family vacation at the world's finest beach—Windy Hill," was the marketing pitch used for these apartments.

Wide beaches are considered family-friendly because the subtle incline decreases the likelihood of a dangerous undertow. A coastal view of Windy Hill Beach shows its wide, flat appearance. Unfortunately for surfers, wide beaches are not good for seeking powerful wave action. However, parents tend to be grateful that wider beaches provide more time to catch a runaway toddler before the child reaches the ocean.

The Grand Strand Motor Lodge creatively used chunks of coquina, locally called mud rock, to form a solid fence culminating with an unusual arched entryway that directed guests to the motor lodge's office. These rocks were sourced from the 1930s excavations of the nearby Intracoastal Waterway and were freely given away during the excavations. During the 1960s, Alfred Williamson was the manager of this Highway 17 motor lodge built of concrete blocks.

This 1960s aerial photograph of Windy Hill Beach and facing north begins in the foreground at Ponderosa and Sherwood Forest campgrounds, advances to Kit's Fishing Pier, and moves farther north to the Windy Hill Beach Fishing Pier, a downtown landmark.

An early view of surf seining at Windy Hill Beach shows sizeable fish on the strand with very few houses in the background. Fishermen are busy collecting their catch from the strand. Eugene Platt was one of several area fishmongers who ran a seasonal seining operation before tourism overtook the north strand beaches.

The 21-unit Lou-Gar Motel, located at 4203 Ocean Boulevard, was operated by Louise Ramsbottom, wife of John Garnett Ramsbottom. She ran this motel from the living room of her neighboring home. Its unique name likely resulted from combining the first syllables of Louise and Garnett. He was a beloved local physician, and she was active in the Garden Club of South Carolina for 45 years.

Fleming's Ocean Court Apartments, owned by Mr. and Mrs. P.K. Fleming, was named the Ocean Court Apartments when Everette and Irene Beaver owned its 31 units at 3805 South Ocean Boulevard, next to the Windy Hill Beach Fishing Pier. Many Grand Strand motels were renamed when ownership changed, perhaps to convey that the enthusiastic new owners would improve

The Mike-Ann Motel and Restaurant on Highway 17, pictured in the 1950s, was managed by Mr. and Ethel Lee Harrell for decades. It had 20 units when this image was created and was open year-round by the 1960s. The origin of the name "Mike-Ann" is unknown.

the guest experience to earn loyalty. The Flemings were a local couple, whereas many guest accommodations were owned by out-of-towners, which reduced the percentage of locally earned tourism dollars that remained in the community to further stimulate its economy.

The Windy Hill Beach Corporation developed Windy Hill and built its fishing pier. The pier was over 1,000 feet long and claimed to be the north strand's oldest pier. Fishing tackle and refreshments were sold in the pier's store, which had red Coca-Cola buttons on its overhead signage.

The name of Long Bay Motel replicates a historic name for the Grand Strand, with its naturally elongated bay. Located beside Kit's Fishing Pier, this motel with "spacious rooms and apartments" was owned and operated by Mr. and Mrs. J.S. Lewis.

Treasure Cove Motor Court on Highway 17 featured 28 ranch-style units, 5 of which had kitchenettes. Its amenities included a large swimming pool, shuffleboard, and badminton, but there was a surcharge for television. D.M. "Pete" Simpson was the motor court's manager around 1964. This pre-1950 motor court was originally advertised with the tagline, "Travel first class for less."

The Fish are Biting at Windy Hill, Ocean Drive Beach, S. C.

Fishing is much more exciting when the fish are biting, so everyone hopes for that rewarding experience. Here, Windy Hill Beach's fishing pier has a fair crowd, indicating that successful catches were happening. The end of this pier is missing, with jagged posts protruding from the ocean, so this image was likely from 1955, after Hurricane Hazel struck the previous October.

Windy Hill Beach, shown in this 1961 picture taken from the Windy Hill Beach Fishing Pier, was so wide that crowding would have been almost impossible. Notable features include sand fencing (to restore sand dunes) and a triangular portable storage unit perched upon the dunes for seasonal storage of beach rental equipment when lifeguards monitored the beaches and rented useful canvas chairs, large umbrellas, and floats to guests.

The oceanfront Tricia Lyn Motel and Apartments at 4601 South Ocean Boulevard had 21 deluxe units beside a heated pool facing the ocean, which was noted as being only 12 feet away. Hubert and Florence Troutman owned and managed this property; it had two fishing piers within two blocks. Mance Watkins later managed the Tricia Lyn, and Charles and Judy Helsel owned it in the 1980s.

Windy Hill Beach's tall dunes provided a protective buffer for oceanfront properties during hurricanes. Mature vegetation covering the dunes indicates that they had remained undisturbed for many years. The width of this beach entryway suggests it was man-made to provide access for lifeguard and emergency vehicles in addition to beach visitors.

Wacky Golf on Highway 17 was a favorite family amusement among miniature golf courses because of its colorful, exaggerated characters. This imitation of an Easter Island statue was painted a sunny yellow. A second Wacky Golf location in Myrtle Beach enabled guests to conveniently play the courses no matter where they were staying along the Grand Strand.

Windy's Pancake House, located on Highway 17 at Forty-eighth Avenue South in the Windy Hill section, was favored by locals and tourists alike. In addition to pancakes, Windy's had a full breakfast menu and served all types of sandwiches from 6:00 a.m. to 2:00 p.m. daily. Pancakes are hugely popular with vacationers, perhaps because most families have little time for daily breakfast preparations at home.

Sherwood Forest Family Campground on the Ocean was a 400-acre recreational accommodation at the southern terminus of Windy Hill. It offered 400 campsites in either forested shade or sunny lots near the shore. Connections for power, water, and sewer were available, as was access to the nearby Kit's Fishing Pier. Howard F. Auman managed this campground around 1970, before it was redeveloped as Ocean Creek Resort.

Ocean Creek and Kit's Fishing Pier are visible in this aerial view that shows portions of the neighboring Sherwood Forest and Ponderosa campgrounds. They were separated by North Myrtle Beach's southern boundary. Camping on the Grand Strand became an accessible, affordable family vacation as more campgrounds opened, leading to the area being named the "Camping Capital of the World."

Ponderosa Family Campground was beside Sherwood Forest Family Campground and immediately south of Windy Hill Beach's town limits. Ponderosa also had 400 campsites, and both campgrounds closed during winter. Around 1970, Guy and Claudine Hammond managed Ponderosa, which had a Western-themed general store named the Trading Post. Ponderosa later closed and was redeveloped as Bay Cove Resort.

The Village of the Barefoot Traders began in the 1970s as six similarly themed shops that soon expanded to 15 stores offering coastal-themed clothing, food, and gifts. This successful shopping mecca on White Point Swash at Highway 17 later expanded again and was renamed Barefoot Landing. This was originally the historic Gause's Swash, where Pres. George Washington spent a night at Gause's Tavern on his 1791 Southern tour.

Politics have impacted the North Myrtle Beach area throughout its history, especially since its 20th-century population explosion. Notable North Myrtle Beach politicians have included US representative John Jenerette, shown here with his former wife, Rita; South Carolina representatives Lloyd B. Bell, Tracy Edge, Ralph Ellis, and John Jenerette; and South Carolina senators Dick Elliott, Ralph Ellis, and Greg Hembree.

After North Myrtle Beach incorporated, Ocean Drive resident Polly Lowman recognized the city needed a newspaper, so she established the *North Myrtle Beach Times* in 1971. She is pictured in July 2019 in the *Times* office with her son, Michael, displaying the Legacy Award she received from North Myrtle Beach. Lowman has served as the *Times'* editor and publisher, sustaining her newspaper's success, for a half century. Now that is a story! (Courtesy of Polly Lowman.)

A Grand Strand sunrise, photographed in 1971 by the author, is indicative of the Atlantic Ocean's majesty and its powerful allure. Regardless of how crowded this coast becomes as it strives to accommodate additional guests and residents, the tides still ebb and flow daily, and the ocean's appearance constantly evolves depending upon the weather and the seasons. Therein lies its powerful attraction, which leads beach visitors to relocate here so they can become anchored to this amazing Atlantic shore.

Visit us at
arcadiapublishing.com

Printed in the USA
CPSIA information can be obtained
at www.ICGtesting.com
LVHW062150100923
757618LV00005B/200